RIZ
Long Blanc

500g

cere

Vivien Paille
COUSCOUS
Grain Moyen

10F20

8F50

QUARTZ AMBRÉ

HOLLY

Parfum POMME VERTE
HOLLYWOOD

Parfum ANANAS
HOLLYWOOD
Chewing Gum
FRUITS DE SAISON

5F00

Sauce América

LES GRANDS CLASSIQUES
Knorr
Poireaux
pommes de terre

Le N° de la chance
10.000F
A GAGNER
TOUS LES MOIS

1 litre

LES GRANDS CLASSIQUES
Knorr
Poule
au vermicelle

Potage
4 assiettes

1 litre

LES GRANDS CLASSIQUES
Knorr
Poireaux
pommes de terre

Le N° de la chance
10.000F
A GAGNER
TOUS LES MOIS

1 litre

5F0

D1292531

VILLAGE VOICES

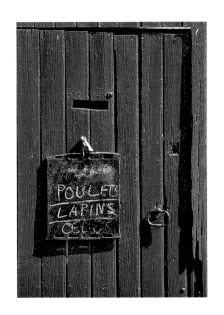

VILLAGE VOICES

FRENCH COUNTRY LIFE

MARIE-FRANCE BOYER

PHOTOGRAPHS BY

SAMUEL DHOTE, ÉRIC MORIN, PIERRE SOISSONS, IVAN TERESTCHENKO

WITH 144 ILLUSTRATIONS, 134 IN COLOUR

Thames & Hudson

FOR GUSTAVE AND LOUIS,

WHO WILL NEVER KNOW THESE NOW-VANISHING PLACES.

DESIGNED BY MICHAEL TIGHE

Translated from the French by Barbara Mellor

Any copy of this book issued by the publisher as a paperback is sold subject to the condition that it shall not by way of trade or otherwise be lent, resold, hired out or otherwise circulated without the publisher's prior consent in any form of binding or cover other than that in which it is published and without a similar condition including these words being imposed on a subsequent purchaser.

First published in the United Kingdom in 1999 by Thames & Hudson Ltd, 181A High Holborn, London WC1V 7QX

© 1999 Thames & Hudson Ltd, London

All Rights Reserved. No part of this publication may be reproduced or transmitted in any form or by any means, electronic or mechanical, including photocopy, recording or any other information storage and retrieval system, without prior permission in writing from the publisher.

British Library Cataloguing-in-Publication Data
A catalogue record for this book is available from the British Library

ISBN 0-500-01945-2

Printed and bound in Singapore by Tien Wah Press

Half-title: a farm door in the department of the Nord.
Page 2: a table set for a wedding feast in the Jura.
Title page: a village square in Provence.
Pages 4–5: the railway station at Vic-sur-Cère in the Auvergne.
This page, background: a bicycle shop in the Charente.

CONTENTS

Once there was the French village. Clustered around the church, the *mairie* (mayor's office) and the village school were the shops and cafés essential for daily life, with fitting names – L'Utile et l'Agréable (Practical and Pretty), A la Confiance (Reliable Stores), Aux Trois Moineaux (The Three Sparrows), or even Cendrillon-Chausseur (Cinderella Shoes) on Rue des Corps-Nus-Sans-Tête (Naked and Headless Bodies Street). These shops enjoyed a relationship with their customers that was founded on trust, on the quality of their merchandise and the dependability of their service. And the daughter of the owner of the hardware shop might be married to the butcher, and the postwoman was perhaps not only the doctor's sister but also the tobacconist's wife. In this claustrophobic, conservative microcosm of a social world, everyone had the measure of everyone else and kept a shrewd eye on their business.

PREFACE

In the villages of isolated rural areas such as the Cotentin peninsula in Normandy, the Jura mountains in East France and the Massif Central, shops like these still exist. Their fittings date back to the war years: unchanging and always harmonious, they were the work of carpenters whose families still live locally. Equipped with counters and tills, shelves and drawers, they are painted in wood-grain effect inside and out, or in a dark brown, or occasionally pale green or sky-blue. Only in the 1970s, when the large retail chains started to impose a uniform style on their outlets throughout France, did new materials begin to make their appearance. The advent of mail-order catalogues has since set the seal on these changes in taste, rendering local influences a thing of the past. As cars have become the most popular means of transport, so people living in rural areas have become accustomed to new ways of shopping.

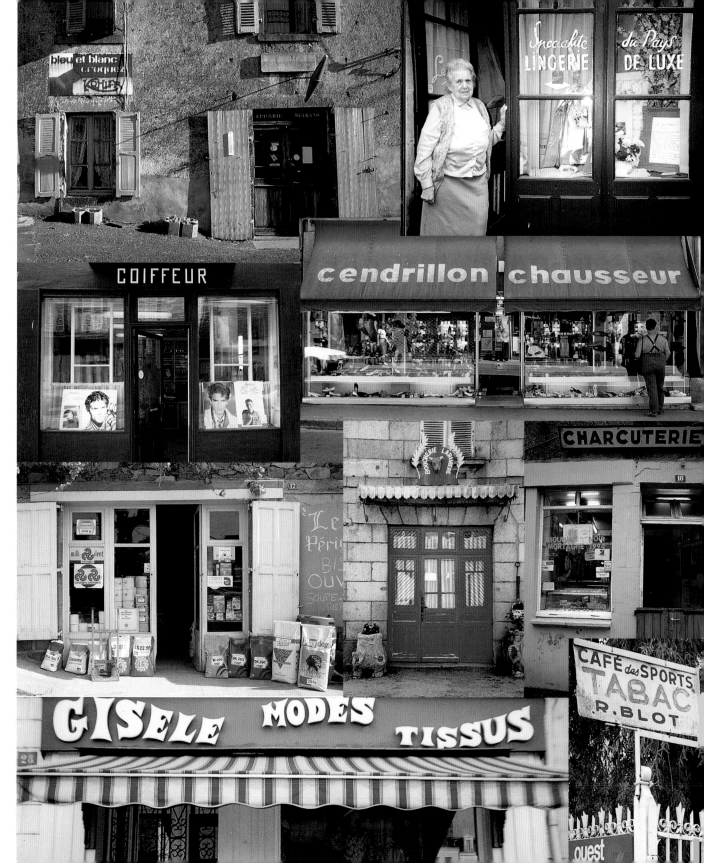

And finally, springing up on the outskirts of towns, the megastores and hyper-markets, DIY stores and the ubiquitous garden centres have arrived to overturn the customs, contacts and shopping habits of rural life. Most village shops have now closed, and those that linger on are the last survivors of a vanished age. Hotels and café-restaurants, ill-adapted to modern health and safety regulations and left high and dry by motorway development, are more or less uniformly modernized. There are very few proprietors now who would have the courage to decorate their walls with a photograph of mountains, or to choose a combination of green and brown flock wallpaper to show off Renoir reproductions and the stuffed head of a deer. Dreamed up with delight, such schemes of decoration breathe an endearing enthusiasm; they have a kitsch appeal which immediately lays them open to sophisticated urban accusations of 'bad taste'. Shop-keepers and the new country dwellers alike aspire to the same bland, conformist approach – the obligatory matt stainless steel, limed oak and shades of grey – the chic-and-simple style waiting in the wings beside minimalism or punk, and electronic shopping around the corner.

So it is that in rural France, two types of villager and two types of decor are found side by side. There are the old, who sometimes live out the end of their lives in a poignant melancholy. The young, the under-forties, locals or refugees from urban life, are fired with amazing dynamism – they run all-purpose shops that sometimes also function as post office or 'Internet service', or take on the post of village mayor or schoolteacher. Finally, a colour-coded army of vans – yellow for the post, blue for *gendarmes*, grey for mobile shops – roams the length and breadth of the great empty spaces of the French countryside, delivering letters or bread, slippers or sausages to their customers, who often see no other visitors.

Page 9: a grocer-tobacconist in the Gers; Madame Léone, specialist in openwork embroidery in the Charente; a hairdresser's shop in Normandy; the Cinderella shoe shop in the Midi; a butcher's shop in the Creuse; a ready-to-wear clothes shop in the Perche… For the moment – but for how much longer? – all these small shops thumb their noses at superstores and electronic shopping. *Opposite*: the inside of a grocer's shop, opened in the Auvergne in 1941, whose owner has never been able to get used to new francs (introduced in 1960).

If French rural life has its strong points, the decor of its restaurant dining rooms is not one of them. This oscillates uneasily between gloomy utilitarianism and trite conventionality. And yet here and there, there are original establishments that remain uninfluenced by the way things are done elsewhere and are ruled instead by the promptings of the heart – where poetically inspired individuals have created warm or witty decors from which two main themes emerge: a reverence for all that is antique, and a celebration of rural life. In order to qualify as antique, the dining room must display a number of common features, including beams, unplastered stone or half-timbered walls, an open fireplace, wrought iron, animal harnesses, warming pans, grandfather clocks, copper utensils and stuffed heads of deer and boar. If there is any furniture, it will be a Henri II dresser or an imposing cupboard.

DÉCOR à la CARTE

The tables are invariably elegantly laid, with cloth and overcloth in white lace or cotton (pink or preferably red) protected by white paper; serviettes (cotton again) folded in the shape of fans, shells, hats, lilies or clover leaves; and pewter stem vases, each holding a sprig of gypsophila and a rosebud. Only the heavy white porcelain dinner plates bearing the restaurant insignia have disappeared.

At the Hôtel de la Paix in the village of Longny (in lower Normandy), Claude Lalaounis has taken matters much further, spending the whole of the 1970s creating the delirious decor of his restaurant. This jovial former chef and 'Companion of the Dish of Tripe' favours a style which might be described as Renaissance revival kitsch.

His only criteria are his own heartfelt passions and aesthetic enthusiasms. There are high-backed, velvet-covered chairs in Henri II style, and a vividly patterned carpet.

14

Page 13: on the wall of a café-restaurant close to the Forest of Lyons in Normandy, a panoramic photograph of a woodland glade provides a background to a stuffed deer's head – a style of decoration highly fashionable in the 1960s. *Right*: during their lunch break these *gendarmes* appreciate a touch of style: white tablecloth, pewter candelabra, seventeenth-century-inspired wallpaper and a painting in the manner of Turner.

The doors are padded and studded, either set in pointed arches picked out with bricks and opening on to secret stairs, or framed by screws from an old wooden press and covered in figured velvet. And this is not the limit of his baroque genius: he has had the cement walls whitewashed and decorated with personal maxims inscribed in a range of imitation stones, incorporating shelves of various dimensions to hold his collections: an array of stuffed animals, including not only peacocks, foxes and stags, but also gannets and cassowaries (which an eccentric neighbour attempted, without success, to breed locally), and an eclectic range of statuary, from plump-cheeked cherubs, Joan of Arc and the Virgin Mary to aged ploughmen, Quasimodo and the gargoyles of Notre-Dame. As for the paintings, the French school of the eighteenth century predominates, with

reproductions of charming compositions by Greuze and Madame Vigée-Lebrun in baroque gilt frames. To impose a note of unity on the decor, candelabra, chandeliers, lace and other trimmings are in abundance, and the ceiling is covered with moquette in a brown and orange pattern, echoing the carpet, framed by triple moulding.

Standing at the crossroads of two major routes in Béarn (in the depths of south-west France), the Auberge des Chênes belongs to the category once known as *routiers*, and serves a clientele of workmen and lorry drivers for whose convenience a little wash-basin has been installed under a stuffed and mounted boar's head. Here they can wash their hands before buying their newspaper – the hotel is also a newsagent's – and seating themselves at a table facing an imitation stone fireplace displaying a set of copper shell cases from the First World War. Another wall is papered with a large panoramic photograph celebrating the splendours of nature – popular in the 1960s.

Opposite above: this café in Savoie boasts a decor dedicated to the glories of nature, with photographs of deer and of a herd of cows, and a reproduction of a famous canvas by the animal painter Oudry. In the Corsican village of Agriate (*opposite, below left*), a wall painting evokes the architecture of the region; in Béarn an imitation stone fireplace shows off First World War shell cases (*left*), and a washbasin (*opposite, below right*), presided over by a boar's head, is set in the middle of the restaurant for lorry drivers to wash their hands before sitting down to eat.

16

The spirit of Renoir presides
happily over these leafy garden
rooms, garlanded with vines
and bamboo, built before the
Second World War behind

a rather forgotten restaurant
between Nancy and Troyes.
A little path leads to the bowers
at the end of the garden, which
spring to life at weekends.

In the Corsican village of Agriate, a local artist has created a gouache mural of old village houses against a *trompe-l'oeil* background of imitation stonework forming the shape of the island. The walls of the banqueting-room of the Auberge du Thuyé in the Doubs are decorated with ten scenes from the agricultural life of the region – including spruce-logging, the gentian harvest and cheese-making – painted by local artist Henri Chappatte in 1970. People come from all over the area to this pretty hamlet in the wooded mountains of the Jura to celebrate birthdays, retirements, christenings and weddings. Chantal and Hervé, a young amateur musician who plays at village dances, plan to celebrate their wedding with a feast for sixty guests, seated at a U-shaped table. They have settled on decorations of pink balloons, doves, fans, garlands and a grand piano made of pink and white tissue paper. The highly elaborate menus wish the happy couple long life and describe the various dishes in lyrical, convoluted fashion: *Fillet of Sea Bass with 'Rambler' Sauce – Woodland Delights in Pastry* (that is, mushroom tart) – *A Mouse's Banquet* (assorted cheeses) – *Pyramid of Happiness* (meringue and chantilly). After the dancing, most of the guests will stay the night ready for the simpler wedding breakfast the following day.

Opposite: in the dining-room of the Hôtel de France at Longny-au-Perche, a door covered with Louis XIV-style moquette trimmed with gold braid is framed by the screws of a wooden press. Beneath a reproduction of a painting by Greuze, the cutlery is stored in a case covered with Genoese velvet.

The Auberge des Tonnelles stands where the River Saulx flows beneath ancient bridges between Nancy and Troyes. Popular in the 1960s, the inn looks dejected now, but behind it are five leafy garden rooms, with sloping roofs and wooden trellises from prewar times, that can hold a hundred guests. The spirit of Renoir and de Maupassant seems to linger, while the aged waitress would not be out of place in a Brueghel painting. She brings oval platters of trout swimming in cream sauce. She smiles; her parents worked here too; you wonder how much longer she can carry on; whether the begonias and dahlias, the bamboos and vines will still be here next time.

In the restaurant at the
Hôtel de France, Claude
Lalaounis – 'Companion of

the Dish of Tripe' – has given
free reign to his penchant for
Renaissance revival kitsch.

Left, right, and overleaf: to celebrate their wedding at the Auberge du Thuyé, in the Haut-Doubs, Chantal and Hervé have chosen a romantic theme in shades of sugar pink. Carnations, dahlias and artificial lace embellish the room, decorated in the 1970s with wall paintings depicting scenes from the agricultural life of the Jura.

With its original till, counters and shelves painted in wood-grain effect and its row of traditional sweet jars, the café-grocer's in the village of Les Pieux, in the north of the Cotentin peninsula, is the very image of a classic general store. Here the Leroy family sells everything imaginable, from sugared almonds, liquorice and toffees ('our answer to the Mars bars and Tic-Tacs sold elsewhere') to tins of haricot beans, mixed vegetables, cassoulet and sardines, not forgetting wine, beer and aperitifs. Dry cat food is right next to brooms, floorcloths, cottonwool, eau de cologne and insecticides, and straw hats jostle for space with pots of flowers, toys, fishing rods and crockery, including the inevitable *poubelles de tables*, the small table waste-bins that are always favourites for wedding gifts. 'My grandfather's aunt started the grocer's shop in the nineteenth century. My grandfather enlarged the shop by taking over the

THE LAST SHOPS

courtyard in 1911, but at that point my grandmother died and he never opened the restaurant he'd planned, so we've stayed as a café and general store.'

On the main square of the village of Boubers-sur-Canche, to the north of Amiens, the Rendez-vous des Pêcheurs (or The Fishermen's Return) proclaims itself a café-*charcuterie*. The owner's daughter serves customers while her father smokes sausages and chitterlings in a courtyard hidden away at the back of the house. Desolate piles of slippers, fishing rods, and tins and jars lie abandoned in another tiny room – the only signs that this was also once a grocer's shop.

Chez Jean, on the main road through the village of Rombies in the Avesnois, used to be a café-hairdresser. The hairdresser is no more, but, since 1953, his widow has continued to offer a welcome, running a bottled-gas depot and selling plant cuttings.

Page 28: the decor of this café-cum-general store in the north of the Cotentin peninsula has not changed since 1911. Through the application of numerous layers of paint, the shop has taken on a uniform brown colour, and it still has its original counter, till and shelves, all in painted wood (*pages 30–31*).

Page 32: a café-hairdresser's on a main road in the department of the Nord. Nowadays the hairdresser's widow (*left*) sells bottled gas, plant cuttings and seeds, but the outdoor men's urinal, installed between zinc panels, is still there.

At Brezolles in the Thymerais, the young Jean-Pierre Penvern displays a clutch of certificates – ranging from one for the region's 'nicest hairdresser' to its 'finest hair-care expert' – between the colour television and a masculine beauty with an immaculate hairstyle. It was Jean-Pierre's father who, in 1941, set up shop behind a frontage of ivory-painted wood, frosted and engraved glass, and ceramic tiles. The clientele is varied, ranging from 'cap and slippers to suit and tie', and while a 'shampoo and cut' may cost from 60 to 120 francs, the price of a 'worker's cut, strand by strand' is fixed at 70 francs. The more frivolous side of life is also addressed at Chez

Gisèle-Modes-Tissus, started in 1904 in the Normandy village of Nogent-le-Rotrou by the grandmother of the present owner, a dressmaker and milliner with fifty-five years of experience who makes her own patterns. In the same spirit are Au Fil d'Ariane (Ariadne's Thread), a little to the north, and Chez Denise at Longny (lower Normandy), where the proprietor offers services ranging from the hire of choirboys' cassocks to sewing 'bachelors' buttonholes'. Gisèle, meanwhile, dresses 'young women who can't find what they want, those on the plump side, and the more mature woman'. 'I might be asked to run up a more eye-catching version of a Chanel suit, for instance, or to make both a bride's gown and the outfits for her wedding guests.'

A new breed of shop is now beginning to emerge, with all-purpose titles such as bar-tobacconist-grocer-newsagent. Situated on a frequently foggy crossroads in the Orne, Au Fil du Temps (As Time Goes By) is just such a general shop, with the recent addition of a banqueting-room. Businesses such as these represent the last pockets of life in these most isolated of rural spots, bypassed by the dense motorway network.

The Levrier workshop in Touraine
– a former haberdashery with walls
painted in the obligatory brown –
is now devoted to the sale of
religious ceramic tiles for children.

The café-*charcuterie* at Boubers-sur-
Canche (*left*) – called the Café des
Pêcheurs – is the haunt of local
fishermen, who meet here for the
presentation of competition cups.

The *patron* is known for his
sausages, which he smokes himself
in the courtyard, and which his
daughter sells in the room at the
back of the café (*preceding pages*).

Here no one is too concerned about the decor. But the children of the establishment, and also perhaps its future, may be glimpsed doing their homework at the tables.

Robert Sargent's shop is in the village of Junhac, in the beautiful mountainous region of the Cantal, empty and remote – the village has 60 inhabitants, the *commune* of which it is the centre some 380. The shop is the meeting-place for local fishing and hunting associations, provides a telephone, and sells licences, sandwiches, drinks, newspapers, bottled gas, cigarettes, seeds, plant cuttings and sweets. It also functions as the village's official post office. Solitary and retiring, Robert Sargent provides a one-man service that is as indispensable to the life of the region as its many mobile shops. These travelling shops divide their time between open-air markets and private deliveries, battling along even the narrowest roads and tracks. In Junhac, the butcher's van comes twice a week, the grocer's once a week, and the dairy-and-cheesemonger's, like the fishmonger's, once a fortnight; the draper's van makes a monthly visit, while the baker comes every other day. The French take their bread seriously. Traditional bakers are scandalized by the plastic-wrapped baguettes delivered to supermarkets at a franc per loaf by the big industrial chains. Corinne Wallet starts her bread deliveries every morning at eight-thirty, returning at five to the shop in the village of Quarouble near Valenciennes. 'The whole enterprise started with my husband's grandfather, Pierre-Auguste, who used to make door-to-door deliveries with his horse. During the war, Gus the bread chap, as they called him, helped out quite a few people. Everyone round here remembers him! He taught my husband his trade.' An attractive woman, not yet thirty, she says: 'I never get upset, I smile, and keep a joke up my sleeve. I park the van and take the bread into the house for the older ones. It's hard work, but I like people.' And so in these brick villages the greyest day begins with the smell of freshly baked bread.

Opposite: at Sabres, in the Landes, the Bréziat family bakes a large batch of bread twice a week. As their shop is very small, they store all the bread in the dining-room.

40

In Normandy, surrounded by
the shop fittings installed by his
father in 1941 – glass-fronted
cabinets and engraved glass doors –
Jean-Pierre Penvern displays his

numerous certificates ranging from
'finest haircare expert' to 'nicest
hairdresser'. The picture hanging
over the door (*above*) was painted
by a German prisoner-of-war as
payment for his haircuts.

Opposite: A travelling van selling dairy products in the Jura, a *charcuterie* van in Corsica, a draper's van in the Charente (with shoes, socks, caps, smocks and work clothes), and, *right*, a baker's van in the Nord. These mobile shops travel the length and breadth of the countryside, also stopping at markets. Corinne drives off from the bakery – in the village of Quarouble – at half-past eight every morning, returning at five o'clock to help her husband with the baking.

Villagers queue in front of a mobile *charcuterie* on a village square in the Charente. It usually stops once or twice a week, like the dairy-and-cheese van; the butcher comes once a week, the baker once a day and the draper only once a month. These mobile shops bring villagers out of their houses and provide an impromptu meeting place. Sometimes, in response to a telephone call from a favoured customer, travelling shopkeepers will stop off at the chemist's to collect medicines which they will drop off at the customer's house.

There are 36,000 *communes* in France. At the head of each is the mayor, representing the state, whose offices in the *mairie* display the obligatory portrait of the President of France and the bust of 'Marianne', symbol of the French Republic. According to a popular nineteenth-century dictum, the *commune* was the nursery of liberty; today, local councillors and mayors (who are frequently women) are often surprisingly young in comparison with an ageing rural population. The more or less symbolic monthly 'salary' to which mayors are entitled (less than 3000 francs for a *commune* of under 500 inhabitants) is proof enough that devotion to the public good is the chief motivation for those willing take on the responsibilities of office (and who do so, moreover, on top of the demands of another job). A fairly vague definition of their powers combined with a lack of public funds

PUBLIC

frequently leads them to make subjective – and sometimes risky – decisions. Paulhac has a population of 511, including 60 farmers. Madame le Maire is forty-two and looks ten years younger. She works as a teacher in a neighbouring town. Her immediate concern is to secure the future of the village grocer's shop by means of a grant – the usual strategy – either from a commercial partner or from some obscure state source. The chief preoccupation of Elisabeth Bouchy-Pommier, Madame le Maire of Lépinas in the Creuse, with a population of 228, is the preservation and use of the local architectural heritage. She has just completed the restoration of the former schoolhouse, and proposes to let it out; already in the summer months it hosts cultural exhibitions. Both *mairies* – in Lépinas and in Paulhac – are outwardly rather austere.

In Moustier-en-Fagne in the department of the Nord, as in L'Esclade on the high plateau of the Cantal, the village school consists of a single class of ten pupils. The teacher lives some distance away and travels in daily. She is not yet thirty, and is modern in her approach. Clad in jeans, she sits surrounded by the children – the traditional rostrum has disappeared, and there is a computer. Today, after a discussion about Picasso, some of the children are drawing and cutting out, while others, clustered around the aquarium, study the 'aquatic environment'. 'Mixed-age classes,' declares one teacher of a class of 28 children at three different levels, 'have their advantages and disadvantages. They are very good for the children, as the younger ones learn from the older ones' lessons, and the big ones help the little ones. But the teachers need two pairs of hands. It's very lively but absolutely killing.'

SERVICES

Some twenty or thirty hamlets may depend on the village, linked to it by poor roads and rutted lanes. Down these, every day, comes the postman, on a bicycle or light motorcycle or in a Renault 4 van, according to the size of the round. In Finistère in Brittany, Madame Guèdes has done her round by motorcycle for the past thirty years. Her saddlebags are stacked precariously high with newspapers, parcels (mostly from mail-order companies), registered mail and *baguettes*. 'When I started out I was supposed to deliver postal orders too, but I couldn't manage it! In those days there was much more personal, hand-addressed mail – from sailors far away or children in town.… Today, it's not fashionable for people to send their feelings by post any more. It's sad. But all the extra circulars and junk mail make up for it!' It is common knowledge locally that she also delivers bread and newspapers to isolated houses.

Page 48: a naive-style granite bust of Marianne, symbol of the Republic, in central France. *Opposite:* the 1950s waiting room of a railway station in the Cantal, with commercial scales made by B. Trayvou, flecked ceramic tiles and a photograph of the station in 1900. Fluorescent green 1990s seating (*left*) is now taking the place of the brown screwed-down seating so typical of the 1970s (*right*).

The post office, which shuts at noon on the dot, plays a central part in village life, providing not only postal and Minitel services (the computerized telephone directory), and sound-proofed telephone booths, but also dealing with deposits and withdrawals from the post office savings bank, and paying out pensions.

Like the yellow post vans, the vans of the local *gendarmerie* – blue with a tricolor sticker – can be seen on even the smallest roads. Responsible to the Ministry of Defence, *gendarmes* are charged with maintaining public order in those *communes* without a police station. G*endarmes* wear a distinctive cap called a *képi.*

Another cornerstone of village life is the local church. In the sacristy the faithful meet the priest, consult the registers of baptisms and marriages, or appoint a day for a remembrance service. Here the priest and his helpers prepare for mass and keep ciboriums, monstrances and other sacred vessels. Priestly vestments nowadays are quietly sober, but many village sacristies still store the old vestments that were in use up to the 1960s. Five colours corresponded to different times of year: red, purple, green, black and white for chasubles and stoles. Surplices and light albs were white, and the curious birettas that are now part of history were black. Some sacristies even boast a *chapier,* a chest with pivoting, semicircular drawers, invented in the seventeenth century for storing *chapes* – stiff and heavy ceremonial vestments richly embroidered with gold thread. Above the silence there floats a smell of faded flowers and hot wax that is so redolent of the centuries-old rites of the Catholic church.

Trains provide the most important link with nearby towns. With their single rattling carriages – doubled or even trebled on Friday nights – the TERs (*trains express régionaux*) travel the length and breadth of remote regions such as the Vercors, the Breton hinterland, Haute-Provence, the Aveyron and Picardy, stopping at stations built at the turn of the century on a scale that now seems out of all proportion.

Preceding pages: Gustave Eiffel-style painted ironwork at the stations of Vic-sur-Cère and Murat (*above*). The station at Landeyrat (*below*) is now closed. Aurillac–Brive-la-Gaillarde, Montluçon–Ussel, Briançon–Gap–Nice, Brest–Quimper… the TER (express regional trains) take children to school and workers to their offices, passing through rural scenes otherwise seemingly lost from view for thirty years or more.

Preceding pages: the *mairie* and school on the outskirts of the village of Junhac, which has a population of 380 inhabitants scattered over the surrounding hills. *Opposite:* the fifteen children at this Puy-de-Dôme primary school, surrounded by herds of cows, are at three different age levels. They work on the computer but still use chalk to write on the blackboard. This covered playground in the Midi (*right*) still sports a climbing rope, with a bell to signal the end of break.

Every style is to be found here, from pre-war brown to 1960s tubular steel and on to the salad-green shades of the 1980s. Large black-and-white photographs of the station buildings surrounded by cows and mountains, hang on the walls like enlargements of old postcards, above painted iron coat hooks. Moulded plastic seats are screwed to the walls. From Vic-sur-Cère (Massif Central), trains take passengers to Aurillac in twelve minutes and to Paris in six hours. As you watch the countryside unfolding between the sunshine-yellow pleated blinds, you get some measure of the isolation of these rural *communes*. The stations have names such as Barsac, Gouzon and Bornel-Belle-Eglise; the TER to Brive-la-Gaillarde also goes through La Roquebrou. The train sweeps past fishermen in waders on the River Cère, while buzzards circle overhead. The river purls against mossy boulders, carries off tree trunks, glides beneath steep banks and ripples along pebbly strands. With its deafening tunnels and its rushing waterfalls, it is astonishingly wild. No path will ever penetrate these woods now coming to life in the April chill, with their ochres and mustard-greens, their purple branches and grey plumes. The train draws to a halt in front of the Hôtel de la Gare, and opposite it are rows of onions in village vegetable gardens. A woman passenger recognizes a countrywoman, a former acquaintance who is also on her way to Brive. 'Now that I'm a widow,' (curled up snail-like on her head is a small black velvet hat), 'I live with my brother. He used to live alone on his farm. He was going to be married, but she fell out of a cherry tree. He said: "Never again." My grandson comes during the holidays, but manners are not what they used to be. Sometimes I'm quite ashamed for him. And yet it's not that he's badly off....' Fifty kilometres later, it is her neighbour's turn; she talks about her garden: 'I've got some fine plum trees, but the fieldmice are nibbling the roots. This year I'm going to try doing some grafts. But I know that's not the problem. It's all in the plumstone.'

The sacristy of the church at Montsalvy (*below right*), the place where sacred vessels are stored, and where the faithful come to talk to the priest about preparations for a christening or a mass in remembrance. *Above:* an eighteenth-century *chapier* (for storing vestments). *Overleaf:* the room in which marriages are celebrated in the *mairie* at Paulhac.

Page 64: Babette, Madame le Maire of Lépinas, officiating at her first marriage in the village. *Page 65:* the *mairie* at Maconcourt. *Left and right*: post offices and *gendarmeries* are often housed in old buildings in the village that have been refurbished. Post vans and *gendarmes'* vans criss-cross the countryside daily. *Gendarmes* are sometimes known to keep photographs of their loved ones – or of some secret dream – inside their caps (their *képis*).

The entrance to this old building, now a post office, provides shelter from the weather in this high, mountainous region when villagers come to collect their pensions or withdraw savings.

ENTREE DU BUREAU

l'éternel féminin

Théâtre Alcyon – Compagnie Patrick Mélior

There is no rational explanation for choosing to stay in hotels that the Michelin guide refuses to favour with a star. To appreciate these hotel bedrooms properly, you need to stumble upon them by accident, to be a romantic, a poet or in love; or else to be spartan in your tastes, for if one quality distinguishes them above all others, it is their notable lack of comfort. Other guests – the regular clientele, consisting largely of labourers employed on local building sites, commercial travellers and families passing through on their way to christenings or funerals – generally have little choice in the matter. Distinguishing characteristics include a naked light bulb suspended from the ceiling, worn linoleum or threadbare fitted carpet on the floor, and a shower shared with other guests – or possibly a plastic shower stall with resonant acoustic qualities, positioned inside the room in such a way that you have to manoeuvre

UNSTARRED
HOTEL ROOMS

yourself round it in order to get from one side of the bed to the other. The mattress has a dip in the middle into which sleeping bodies subside, for better or worse, but it rests on a charming wooden *lit bateau*, a painted iron bedstead topped with copper balls or a Henri II Renaissance-style confection with matching wardrobe and table.

Opposite the bed, beside a window looking out over wooded hills, or rocks topped by a lighthouse, or a murmuring stream, stands the celebrated white ceramic duo of washbasin and bidet. Sometimes the bidet pivots so that you can push it back against the wall, or it might be made of enamel and wedged under the washbasin on an X-shaped metal frame. This ineffably French accessory haunts the nation's imagination, and was an object of fascination for turn-of-the-century photographers, on a parallel with innumerable studies of women after the bath by painters such as Degas and Bonnard. Picturesque or erotic, the bidet may be viewed – for those susceptible to its charms – as part of the armoury of love.

But all this notwithstanding, nothing in these modestly priced rooms (from 130 to 220 francs) would be impossible to bear if one could only change their dimensions (up to fifty square metres) or their wall coverings. Little attic rooms with wood-panelled walls and plump red eiderdowns do exist, certainly. But the general rule seems to dictate that vast expanses of wall should be covered with 1950s wallpaper, dotted with either little *toile de Jouy*-type landscape scenes against a white, yellow or beige background, or a discreet floral pattern anticipating by many years the triumph of the Laura Ashley style. A more 'modern' approach – in other words, dating from the 1970s – features embossed wallpaper with a subtly iridescent pattern of bamboo and rushes, nicely set off by a section in Louis-the-whatever revival stripes. For reasons of hygiene, the wall around the washbasin is protected with a sheet of adhesive plastic in a co-ordinating colour scheme: brown checks for beige rushes, blue foliage for blue flowers – but never green, which 'brings bad luck'. The curtains, if there are any, add a fanciful note with a third pattern (floral), or limit themselves more soberly to the braid-trimmed cotton satin, with or without pelmet, so dear to the 1960s; they generally hang partly over the stout cast-iron radiators which from October to April struggle in vain against the arctic cold. The interiors of these hotels have often remained unchanged since the nineteenth century, and their very names seem immutable: Hôtel Moderne, Terminus, du Centre, de France, de Paris, de la Gare, de la Poste, au Lion d'Or, au Chapeau Rouge, or des Trois Ecus.

Page 70: herds of cattle customarily pass between the church and this inn in the Jura. You can hear the tinkling of the cowbells from your room. *Opposite:* unstarred hotels in the Charente, Franche-Comté, Brittany and the Aubrac: these establishments provide a room for the night for passing workers, walkers and the occasional impecunious eccentric. The rooms decorated in blue, with their Henri II-style furniture (*bottom right*), have recently been brought into line with current health and safety regulations.

Once they were rather smart, and bustled with life. Nowadays, to reach your room with its musty aroma of frying, furniture polish and mothballs, you trail along twisting corridors, up and down steps, and across landings boasting a wardrobe, a piano adorned with a vase of artificial flowers, or faded gold-framed reproductions of paintings by Rubens, Renoir or Vermeer, all the while clutching a large key which eventually rattles loosely in the lock. The telephone, if it is not beside the toilets, is next to the reception desk where you are forever having to move to let visitors pass and a private conversation is out of the question.

These *hôtels de préfecture,* their decoration dating from a forgotten era before the advent of modern tourism with its strict rules of hygiene and associated costly renovations, are vanishing one by one in the face of new demands from both clients and the authorities. 'We have two years to conform to the new standards,' explain their owners. The mayor is responsible for 'safety', and the local fire brigade for fire precautions. A hotel without stars must contain

Preceding pages: a hotel room in Burgundy, decorated with flowery wallpaper and overlooking a kitchen garden. *Opposite:* with its braid-trimmed lampshades and curtains, and its vintage sanitary ware installed opposite the bed and between the windows, this old coaching inn on the Cotentin peninsula exhales an old-fashioned elegance, more provincial than rural. *Left:* an attic bedroom in an inn near Morteau, with walls panelled with varnished wood and a plump cherry-red eiderdown on the bed.

at least five rooms – seven square metres for singles, eight square metres for doubles – with shutters at the windows and floors insulated for sound, though fire-resistant materials are required only in communal areas. The owners of these isolated hotels are often badly informed or are the victims of arbitrary local regulations. Not realizing that they are exempt from regulations applying to 'places of public passage', they opt for a complete and expensive refurbishment from top to bottom. Or else they simply close their doors. Vulnerable and intimate, these unique establishments are even now being consigned to oblivion.

Right: bucolic wallpaper in the Aveyron. *Opposite:* beds in carved wood and in metal painted to look like wood, both bought before the war in the neighbouring towns of Brive-la-Gaillarde or Aurillac. The ubiquitous candlewick bedspreads are steadily replacing traditional floral-printed cretonne. The wall-lights are a 1960s addition.

The soft tones of *toile de Jouy*-style wallpaper in central France (*below centre*), contrast with the stronger shades favoured in the south. On the wall, a 1960s frosted glass wall-light; beside it, a 1950s coat-stand with multicoloured balls in Corsica. *Overleaf:* wainscoting, wardrobes, doors and ceilings in varnished veneer, with 1940s ceiling lights.

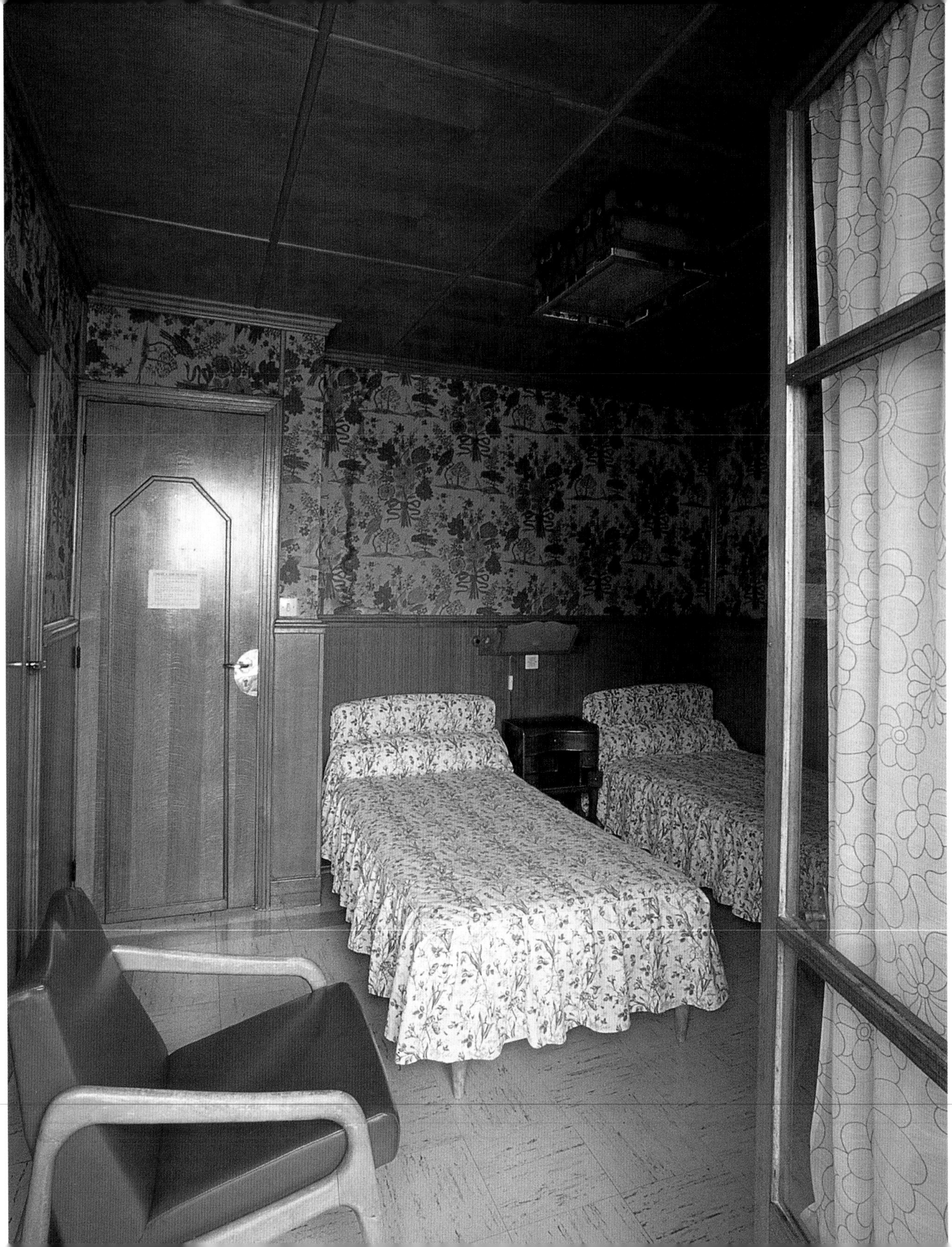

Saved by nostalgia, flourishing still and barely affected by the large agricultural co-operatives, ironmongers' shops are the only traditional businesses to have resisted the march of time. Many of them still retain their turn-of-the-century decor, and some have not only absorbed the functions of the hardware shop and the paint merchant, but have also taken over the role of plumber and electrician. This enables them to increase the range of their stock while still selling their traditional 'household goods' – crockery, saucepans and gifts – as may be seen in typical examples at Aurillac (the Cantal), Bricquebec (Normandy) and Lavaveix-les-Mines (the Creuse). Some of these shops remain faithful to their original function as suppliers for local activities, such as fishing, livestock farming or small industries. They also commission local craftsmen for specific regional items, and are delighted to dispense technical advice.

MALE PF

Madame Ginette Clare runs a shop offering 'general supplies to sailors and oyster farmers' in Rochefort, a small town on the Charente mainland facing the Ile d'Oléron. She is carrying on the business started from scratch by her parents-in-law in 1939: 'Full of curiosity and energy, they did their research in the ports as well as in books, and built up a fine reputation.' Madame Clare married their only son, and together she and her husband ran a shop in Paris selling leather goods. 'My parents-in-law were born business people, like me. They would work their fingers to the bone to introduce new ideas. When my father-in-law died twenty years ago, I took over the business out of family pride and a sense of duty. I decided to leave all as it was. The entire stock is on display, suspended from nails, chains or string. It's not very pretty, but it's got an old-fashioned feel, and for sixty years now people have liked it. They come in out of curiosity, but they never leave without buying something!' Madame Clare (now widowed) takes a pride in her special items of stock, such as oyster picks (for levering oysters off rocks), clam knives and hooks, cockle rakes and crab rods (for rooting under stones for crabs). She sells a great many fishing nets purely for decoration, as well as those 'equipped with the metal alarms required for their use', and landing-nets for sole, plaice, eels and prawns. For boats, she stocks shackles, anchors, bottle screws and pear-shaped rigging eyelets called 'thimbles'. The shrimp baskets are made from wicker or plastic, the marsh baskets from chestnut and metal, and the *galoches*, or sailors' clogs, from wood and leather, complete with their *croumirs*, black felt inner socks with a leather sole. The even wider range of goods on sale at the Chansigaud ironmongers at Saint-Martin-de-Ré (on the Atlantic coast)

ESERVES

features supplies for local shore-fishing, including the curious brass carbide lamps some fishermen attach to their belts for night fishing, guaranteed to 'last out the tide'. In Allanche, on a high plateau of the Auvergne, cattle-farming reigns supreme. The third-generation village ironmonger has a clientele as particular as that in the Charente: a farmer preparing a prize animal for show is quite likely to spend up to 1500 francs on a hand-tooled leather bell-harness with copper decorations, all made by local craftsmen, down to the bell clapper forged by an old blacksmith. To stop calves suckling, a saddler contrives bizarre-looking contraptions worthy of an S&M fetishist. Also on sale are astonishing tiny red plastic masks, sold by weight, and adapted to fit like spectacles over the beaks of aggressive hens to stop them attacking other birds, 'if you don't want to put their eyes out, which is also quite effective'.

Preceding pages: an ironmonger's shop in the village of Le Russey in the Doubs, specializing in tools for do-it-yourself and light agricultural work; the stock includes bilberry rakes, 'hot-water balls', enamelled billy-cans, pots used for sterilizing and brushes for scrubbing out milkcans (*opposite*).

The ironmonger's shop in Allanche (*right*), a small town in the Auvergne where important livestock markets take place, supplies the needs of livestock breeders, including cowbells, nose-rings for bulls, contraptions for stopping calves from suckling their mothers' milk and plastic 'spectacles' for aggressive hens. Both shops have been in existence for three generations.

In the village of Le Russey in the Doubs, close to the Swiss border, Madame Cheval also represents a third generation of ironmongers – the shop opened in 1934 in the old schoolhouse. For forty years she has supplied villagers with the traditional equipment for mushroom- or bilberry-picking in the surrounding mountains, for making preserves, for gardening, or for running a smallholding with two or three animals.

But if only one of all these village places were to survive, it would have to be the garage. Source of all passion and every kind of irrational behaviour, it is to the village men as the hairdresser's is to the women. As one customer diffidently explains: 'I'd broken down, and the garage owner dropped everything to bail me out, as the car

was full of supplies for my restaurant. In two ticks he'd solved the trouble. To thank him, I invited him to supper!' Even more extreme is the customer who pays the garage a sort of monthly retainer for the upkeep of his beloved old car: 'First he said he was the only one who could get the right parts, thanks to his special contacts; then he convinced me he could offer me the cheapest service, then advised me to pay over the odds for complete peace of mind. Finally, since the repairs were never finished on time, he used to lend me his red convertible! For a while I thought it was great, and then I worked out that I was paying a small fortune, and that was the end of it ….' The garage interior, with its glass walls and its organized chaos of spanners, fan belts, tap-and-die sets and wrenches for loosening stubborn nuts, is a source of perennial fascination. Outside, abandoned vehicles lie strewn about like the carcases of giant beasts, and customers refer to their cars as 'she', as though discussing a mare with a blacksmith of an earlier century.

At Ars-en-Ré in the Vendée, Dominique Neveur has taken over Cycles et Pêche, the bicycle and fishing shop that was set up years ago by her parents. These days, the hire and repair of holidaymakers' bikes has taken over from the fishing-reels and live bait proudly trumpeted on the shop's advertisement.

The village garage enjoys virtually mythical status, and car owners almost invariably spend – or waste – far more time there than they mean to. Visible for miles away from its location beside a major road, or hidden behind a row of petrol pumps, housed in a glass-and-metal hangar, tucked away behind a cluster of houses on a road leading nowhere, the village garage is typically strewn with the shells of tractors, Renault 4s, Vedettes and Panhards, and patrolled by barking dogs.

Preceding pages and right: at Rochefort in the Charente, Madame Clare specializes in supplies for river-fishing. Like her parents-in-law, who owned the business before her, she is indefatigable in introducing new ideas, but refuses to make any changes to the original decor. *Opposite:* spoon net for scooping fish from the bottom of nets, chestnut basket for collecting shellfish, and clogs made of wood and leather with their *croumirs*, or felt inner socks.

Only regulars frequent that special breed of café – now fast disappearing – run by the *patron* or *patronne* in their own home. In the hamlet of Bizot in the Jura mountains, the café owned by seventy-seven-year-old 'la' Colette has a licence no. IV, which means she is allowed to serve alcohol. It is a matter of outrage to her, on the other hand, that she can no longer sell a slice of bread and butter, an omelette or a sandwich to hungry travellers passing through, as she has throughout her life in the fine sixteenth-century former courtroom that serves as the café. 'Since 1966, under the new hygiene regulations, I can't keep my sausage or eggs for more than three days! I would have to build large cold stores. I give up....' But she still serves the local gentian liqueur, *absinthe*, coffee and Martini at the top of a dimly lit Renaissance staircase which until 1950 led up to the family grocer's shop and restaurant.

THE CHARM OF

At Azincourt (site of the Battle of Agincourt), in the department of the Nord, Marie Tétard has only to get up from her armchair beside the cooker to serve her customers. She loves to chat while hanging out her washing, a favourite topic being the English and their behaviour in the village, from the Hundred Years' War to the present day.

Since customers no longer come to the café at Gestas, in the Béarn in south-west France, the family will not be renewing its licence no. IV, still fixed above the door, half-hidden by roses. It is now the only indication that this was once a public place.

At Thérondels in the Aveyron, the wine merchant keeps his wine barrels and serves his customers in a barn beside the main road. In the house attached to the barn is the Café Mayniel where customers pay for their wine and drink a glass next to the cooker on which the owner's mother is preparing a sauté of veal with white haricot beans.

A half-knitted cardigan lies on the planewood table, which was made by a local carpenter. Through the window can be seen the white peaks of the Cantal.

In the Breton village of Plounerin, three frozen builders in cement-encrusted dungarees have sought refuge in Jeanne's kitchen, where *la patronne*, in her slippers, makes 'coffee' from chicory for them. They are not local, but everyone knows they are finishing off the doctor's house, that they are lodging nearby and that they don't have a car. Madame Boudet runs a grocer's shop in the Auvergne, Madame Destruhaut a haberdashery in the Landes in south-west France; they both live over the shop, springing up as if from nowhere at the slightest tinkle of the bell on the shop door. Pierrette Destruhaut could not install a stove in her shop until 1968: 'My father wouldn't allow it because of the fire risk. He started running the shop in 1929, and I had to wait until

THE 'BACK ROOM'

he died before I could do it.' She divides her time between her armchair and a back room where she prepares her meals and pots up cuttings. 'Papa sold fabrics and work clothes.' Pierrette still sells Basque linen goods, berets and *sandales* – the proper name for the Basque *espadrilles* – but now assorted gifts also crowd the shelves, providing a little extra at the end of the month. Madame Boudet, her senior by many years, has run her shop in a mountain village of the Massif Central since 1941, though she still can't get used to new francs (introduced in 1960). She stocks tins of cassoulet and petits pois, oil and sugar, soap and sweets. She opens at six in the morning so that local farmers can bring in their fresh milk, for which she can always find customers; then at twelve noon on the dot she shuts up shop and dozes off; on the local radio an accordion bursts into life, but Madame Boudet's hearing is not what it used to be….

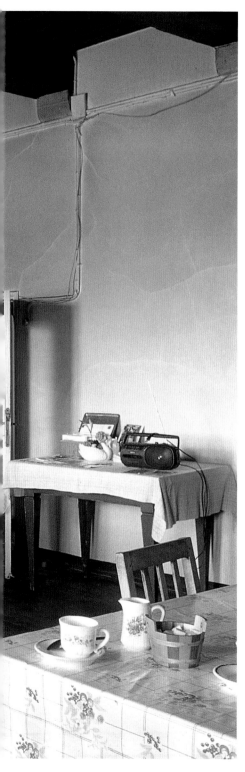

At the wine merchant's in the village of Thérondels in the Aveyron (*preceding pages*), customers are offered a drink in the café-cum-kitchen, as at Gestas in Gascony (*centre right*). *Opposite:* 'la' Colette's café in the Jura is housed in a former courtroom dating from the sixteenth century. At the age of seventy-seven, Colette still serves the local *anis* (an aniseed-based aperitif) from Pontarlier (*below right*), along with the local gentian liqueur 'to aid digestion'. *Above right:* Marie Tétard in her café with a regular customer.

Preceding pages: Marie Tétard's café in the Nord, with its wood-grain paint, its superannuated wallpaper, its lacy frieze and its collection of souvenirs.
Opposite: in the room opening on to the garden behind her

haberdashery shop in the Landes, Pierrette Destruhaut cooks her meals and pots up cuttings between serving customers.
Left and above: this farm in the department of the Nord still sells milk direct to private customers.

Preceding pages and left: whenever the bell on the door rouses her from her gentle doze, Madame Boudet, the *patronne*, makes her unhurried way from her kitchen (*right*) to her shop. Virtually nothing in her house has changed since 1941 – only the stove is new. Though she now prefers to watch the television, Madame Boudet has never been able to bring herself to throw out her old transistor radio.

ACKNOWLEDGEMENTS

My thanks go first and foremost to my friends
Ivan and Pierre, Eric and Samuel, without whom this
book would not have been possible.

Bip and Bobo, M.F. Bouchaud, Alexandre Cammas,
Catherine Carrier, Jean Chouty, Vincent Dané, S. Durin,
Claude and Alain Fassier, Marijke Heuff, A. Le Trouher,
Jean Mortier, Vincent Prache, Philippe Renaud,
Françoise Teynac

PHOTOGRAPHIC CREDITS

Marie-France Boyer: 9 *top (right)*, *centre (below middle) and below (left and right)*; 48; 55; 66 *centre (middle) and below (left and right)*; 73 *top (left and right), centre (above left) and below (middle and right)*.   **Samuel Dhote**: 1; 32; 33; 36–37; 38; 39; 44; 61 *above*; 66 *above (middle) and centre (left)*; 103 *above*; 104–105; 106; endpapers   **Eric Morin**: 3; 6; 9 *centre (above right)*; 14–15; 17 *below left*; 34; 35; 45 *above (right) and below*; 46–47; 58 *above*; 66 *centre (right) and below (middle)*; 67; 80 *above*; 81 *above*; 82; 83; 94; 95; 96; 97   **Pierre Soissons**: 4–5; 9 *above (left) and centre (below left)*; 10; 13; 17 *above*; 50; 51; 52–53; 56–57; 58 *centre and below*; 59; 61 *below*; 62–63; 66 *centre (post office)*; 73 *below (left) and centre (left)*; 74–75; 78; 79; 80 *below centre*; 81 *below*; 88 *above (left), centre (right) and below (middle)*; 89; 92; 93; 100; 101; 108–109; 110; 111   **Ivan Terestchenko**: 2; 9 *centre (above left and below right)*; 16; 17 *(below right)*; 18; 19; 21; 22; 23; 24; 25; 26–27; 28; 30–31; 41; 42; 43; 45 *above (left)*; 65; 66 *above (left and right)*; 68–69; 70; 73 *centre (right and below left)*; 76; 77; 86–87; 88 *above (right), centre (left and middle) and below (left and right)*; 102; 103 *centre and below*; 107; 112

TWO MUSEUMS THAT MUST BE VISITED

Musée du textile et de la vie sociale, 59612 Fourmies, Tel. 03 27 60 23 88.   Musée de l'épicerie, Lignerolles, 61190 Tourouvre, Tel. 02 33 25 91 07.